In Pieces

Samuel Fugate

BookLeaf Publishing

India | USA | UK

Presentation by *BookLeaf Publishing*

Web: www.bookleafpub.com

E-mail: info@bookleafpub.com

ISBN: 9789357215619

First edition 2022

In Time

Truth be told you're the same as all the ones
before,
I put my hand and then my heart in yours,
With all of me I loved all of you.
You stole a piece of me and ran,
But that piece is what makes you different than
all the ones before.

I miss you, and I wish it ended differently,
I'm not over you and I don't know when I will
be,
But I don't need you
And I don't want you.
Knowing that, I still wish it could have been
different.

It's been over for a while now and there isn't
much to say.
That was what you told me, but who am I to
blame?
You for tearing me apart?
Or me for letting you?
I'll get over you in time but for now, there still
isn't much to say.

Walls

I thought that you were mine
Now honestly I'm not fine,
I found love at the wrong time.

I should have never let you in
We were never anything,
I wasted so much on something that had never
been.

All you were was a headache,
All you were was a heart brake.
Just a regret and a mistake.

But I wouldn't trade our time together,
Even if it didn't last forever.
Parting ways was likely for the better.

I just didn't want to see
The walls between you and me.
I couldn't tear them down, then you set me free.

Another Bend

3

River how do you continue to flow?
Steady on you always go;
Always moving on with no home.
Do you never feel alone?

Do you not yearn to get to the end,
To never cross another bend?
Are you okay, or do you just pretend
That it's alright to be nothing more than friends?

From You to Me

I stand on the banks looking out on the river
And I'm reminded of how beautiful the world
can be.
I feel the warmth of the sun and the chill of the
wind,
But beyond these things I see
The grief and yearning of isolation,
Of being separated by impossible boundaries.
With tears in my eyes I look to my left,
There's a bridge and again I'm chilled by the
breeze.
I'm reminded that you can never feel warmth if
you've never been cold,
That you can never feel loved without feeling
grief.
And bridges are built not born,
So maybe one day we can build a bridge from
you to me.

More than You could Give

I hate that you're a memory,
Something in my head that used to be.
At one point you were so real to me,
That I lost track of truth and fantasy.

I wanted more than you could give;
You wanted something else instead.
I let you get inside my head
And when you left I had to find another way to
live.

Ever since, I'd been a drunken fool
Always sat here on a stool.
Beer and liquor were the only tools
That I could find to forget about you.

It will pass, they always said.
But every day I seemed to relive,
The hurt and grief I tried to forget.
And when it didn't pass, I just got used to it.

Remain

I gave up on you and found myself
Almost as I was, but colder.
Who's to say if I learned a lesson?
But I pray that I am stronger.

Yesterday was never even real
Except in tinted memories.
Why was I a fool for you so long?
I put my love for you over my love for me.

Hopefully you are truly gone now,
Gone from my heart, body, and soul.
How were you so embedded in me?
Finally I've got back what you stole.

Not fully alive but not yet dead
Here I still am, alone again.
Will I find a new reason to live?
Either way I will remain.

All of Me

All of me I gave to you,
But we were never meant to be.
Anything at all I would've done for you,
With everything you said I could never see
That I was wrong for you,
And you were wrong for me.

I found my peace in you
While we were laying there together.
My whole heart I gambled on you,
And I wish we could've lied there forever.
But it's best to follow the truth,
Even if it leaves your heart severed.

Spirit

All it takes is one moment
And those memories flood my soul.
A single thought and I relive a lifetime.
You broke my heart but not my spirit,
But what's a spirit when I'm alone?

Joy

Loneliness
With friends or by myself,
When I'm sick or in perfect health,
When I stop to think, I'm always alone.

Grief,
Whether my spirits are high or low,
Whichever direction the wind might blow,
Grief never leaves me.

In the midst of sorrow, joy arises.
Like winter comes around to remind us
To love more freely and care more deeply,
So too does joy and peace,
Comes when we're left in pieces.

Human

I've been blessed and didn't know it,
I've been stressed and didn't show it.

I've been curt when I was needed,
I've been hurt when I was unneeded.

Being human, I can only do so much,
Being human, that is my crutch.

Again

Finally again I think I can feel
All that I lost, has again become real.
It took time to begin to heal,
Until someone stepped in and broke the seal
To my heart and my soul, that I had concealed.

A Beautiful Seed

In fertile ground a seed was planted,
Forgotten about and never tended,
But through many years
The seed persisted.
Someone saw amidst the weeds,
A beautiful flower from a beautiful seed.

Time and Space

Before memory
And beyond fantasy.
Independent of time and space;
Here we are alone together in the face
Of all our adversity,
And all our tragedies.

Somewhere

Somewhere to hide from the rain,
That's all I've ever been.
Something to satisfy an urge
Or a distraction from your pain.
You said maybe that would change,
That you were different,
But it all ended the same.

Pure and Simple

15

Love is pure and love is simple,
But life is unfair and life is fickle.
She gives and she takes,
She loves and she hates,
At her own pace,
And in her own ways.
So don't grow too fond
And don't love too strong.
In the end,
When your ship comes in,
You'll have to cast that teacup away.

Someone to Love

Someone to cling to
Someone to lean to,
Someone to cherish
And someone to love.
Above all else, that's what I crave
Someone to take with me to my grave.

Light is the Color

17

Light is the color of my lover's eyes,
But heavy is the sorrow to bear.
Gentle are the words of my lover,
But harsh are the memories.
I hope for a brighter tomorrow,
To feel the warmth of a burning love;
But I dread the next night.

Where Saints have trod

Where Saints have trod we like our feet to plod.
To follow man as he follows God.
Many false spirits would lure us away,
And we would find ourselves at midnight
spirited away.

www.ingramcontent.com/pod-product-compliance
Lightning Source LLC
La Vergne TN
LVHW050312200726
843509LV00015B/3291